IRONCLADS
THE MONITOR VS THE MERRIMAC
AT WAR

ABNETT • WAGNER • VERMA

OSPREY
GRAPHIC
HISTORY

First published in Great Britain in 2007 by Osprey Publishing,
Midland House, West Way, Botley, Oxford OX2 0PH, UK
443 Park Avenue South, New York, NY 10016, USA
E-mail: info@ospreypublishing.com

A CIP catalog record for this book is available from the British Library

ISBN: 978 1 84603 053 6

Page layout by Osprey Publishing
Map by The Map Studio
Originated by United Graphics Pte Ltd, Singapore
Printed in China through Bookbuilders

07 08 09 10 11   10 9 8 7 6 5 4 3 2 1

FOR A CATALOG OF ALL BOOKS PUBLISHED BY OSPREY PUBLISHING
PLEASE CONTACT:

NORTH AMERICA
Osprey Direct, c/o Random House Distribution Center, 400 Hahn Road,
Westminster, MD 21157
E-mail: info@ospreydirect.com

ALL OTHER REGIONS
Osprey Direct UK, P.O. Box 140 Wellingborough, Northants, NN8 2FA, UK
E-mail: info@ospreydirect.co.uk

www.ospreypublishing.com

CONTENTS

WHO'S WHO

Flag Officer Franklin Buchanan (1800–1874) was commander of the Confederate ironclad warship, *Merrimac* (also known as *Virginia*). He led successful attacks on the Union ships but was wounded and left the *Merrimac* the day before the battle with *Monitor*.

Lieutenant John L. Worden (1818–1897) was the original commander of *Monitor*, leading the ship into the historic battle between the iroclads at Hampton Roads. Worden was wounded during the fighting.

Lieutenant Catesby ap Roger Jones (1821–1877) was executive officer of *Merrimac* and took command of the warship during its battle with the *Monitor* when Flag Officer Buchanan was injured.

Lieutenant Samuel Dana Greene (1840–1884) was executive officer (second in command), of *Monitor* and took charge of the ship after Lt. Worden was injured during the battle between *Monitor* and *Merrimac*.

THE AMERICAN CIVIL WAR 1861-1865

The economic and political differences between the Northern and Southern states in America had become very serious by the middle of the nineteenth century. The biggest difference was over the issue of slavery. The South depended upon slaves to work the plantations that grew crops such as tobacco and cotton. Slavery was illegal in the North. Over the years, many laws were passed to deal with this issue, but none of the laws satisfied both sides.

In 1860, Abraham Lincoln, an anti-slavery candidate, won the presidential election. The South was angered. South Carolina then seceded, or left, the Union. More Southern states seceded. They formed the Confederate States of America, a separate government.

Tensions continued to grow. Finally, on April 12, 1861, Southern forces bombed Fort Sumter, in South Carolina. For the next four years, the North and South battled one other in a conflict that changed the way wars would be fought: the American Civil War would give birth to the age of the ironclad warship. ∎

THE BIRTH OF IRONCLADS

To pay for the costs of fighting the Civil War, Southern states had to continue selling and trading their agricultural crops, such as cotton, overseas. To export cotton, the South had to ship it across the Atlantic Ocean.

The South needed a strong navy to make sure that its trade ships could safely leave Southern ports and make the voyages to Europe and other places. Early in the war, Confederate forces took control of naval bases in the South that had belonged to the United States government. There, they began to rebuild some of the ships they captured.

But the North also began building a strong navy. The federal government already had warships based in the North, and they added

▲

The Union navy used their ships to block the Mississippi River and other water routes. This was done to stop Confederate ships from transporting supplies to their armies. (Courtesy of Casemate)

all kinds of vessels to their navy. Many ships were refitted for battle purposes.

Many Union and Confederate ships were old, wooden sailing ships. The Union navy used many of these vessels in blockades to prevent Southern trade ships from leaving ports in the Atlantic Ocean. If the blockades were successful, Southern trade ships would be kept out of action, and the South's finances would be badly hurt.

This would make it very difficult for the Confederacy to continue fighting the war. To combat the blockades and continue to use the Atlantic trade routes, the Confederacy needed stronger ships with better weapons. The Confederates had to find a way to build fewer, more efficient ships.

In April 1861, the Confederates took control of the Federal Navy Yard at Norfolk, Virginia. Weeks later, they made plans to rebuild the Northern-built *Merrimac*, a steam frigate, which the Union had scuttled before they left the yards. The Confederates rebuilt the vessel and renamed it *Virginia*. Half of the upper hull was cut away and

▲

The Union began to build their own ironclad, the USS *Monitor*, (its crew are shown here on the deck) when they heard rumors of the CSS *Virginia* being built. (NARA)

The Confederate ironclad CSS *Virginia*, was converted from an abandoned wooden Union ship, USS *Merrimac*. (Courtesy of SMH)

▼

fitted with armor. Commanded by Franklin Buchanan, the *Virginia* was the ironclad ship the Confederates hoped would terrorize the Union navy and break the blockade.

The Union was also making plans to build its own ironclad. In October 1861, Swedish engineer John Ericsson agreed to build an ironclad for the North. His creation, *Monitor*, was a remarkable engineering feat. Five inches of armor plating cover its hull and eight inches of armor covered the turret box. Its revolving turret allowed the *Monitor* to fire its two cannons in almost any direction.

With the development of these two technological marvels, the stage was set for one of the greatest sea battles in history.

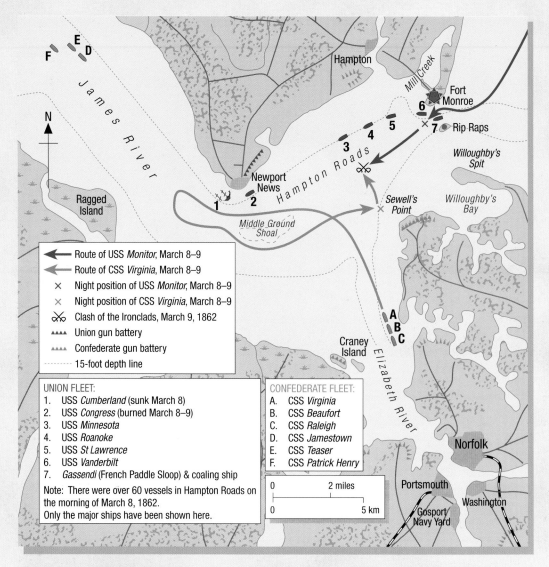

Route of USS *Monitor*, March 8–9
Route of CSS *Virginia*, March 8–9
× Night position of USS *Monitor*, March 8–9
× Night position of CSS *Virginia*, March 8–9
⚔ Clash of the Ironclads, March 9, 1862
▲▲▲▲ Union gun battery
▲▲▲▲ Confederate gun battery
--------- 15-foot depth line

UNION FLEET:
1. USS *Cumberland* (sunk March 8)
2. USS *Congress* (burned March 8–9)
3. USS *Minnesota*
4. USS *Roanoke*
5. USS *St Lawrence*
6. USS *Vanderbilt*
7. *Gassendi* (French Paddle Sloop) & coaling ship

Note: There were over 60 vessels in Hampton Roads on the morning of March 8, 1862.
Only the major ships have been shown here.

CONFEDERATE FLEET:
A. CSS *Virginia*
B. CSS *Beaufort*
C. CSS *Raleigh*
D. CSS *Jamestown*
E. CSS *Teaser*
F. CSS *Patrick Henry*

0   2 miles
0   5 km

WAR AT SEA

On March 8, 1862, the great showdown began as the *Virginia* sailed into Hampton Roads, *Virginia*, a harbor at the mouth of the James River. Comically referred to as "a floating barn roof," the *Virginia* wasted no time showing that its new ironclad technology was nothing to laugh at.

Supported by several other Confederate vessels and with Flag Officer Buchanan in command, the *Virginia* destroyed a Union fleet of wooden warships off Newport News,

The battle between the ironclads USS *Monitor* and CSS *Virginia* (previously the *Merrimac*) is also known as the battle of Hampton Roads. On March 8, *Virginia* attacked a Union blockade and sank the USS *Cumberland* and the USS *Congress*. The next day, *Monitor* entered the conflict and attacked *Virginia* in the first-ever clash of ironclad warfare.

Virginia, in about five hours. The powerful *Virginia* quickly took care of the USS *Cumberland* and *Congress*. During the battle action, another Union vessel, the frigate *Minnesota*, ran aground. The *Virginia*'s overwhelming firepower, protective iron

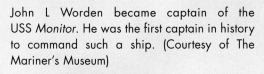

John L Worden became captain of the USS *Monitor*. He was the first captain in history to command such a ship. (Courtesy of The Mariner's Museum)

Flagship Officer Franklin Buchanan commanded the CSS *Virginia* during her attack on the USS *Cumberland* and USS *Congress*. (Courtesy of the Library of Congress)

armor, and devastating battering ram had dished out plenty of punishment to the shocked Union forces.

But later that night, the Union's *Monitor*, commanded by Lieutenant John Worden, arrived in the area. The next morning, crowds of Union and Confederate supporters watched the developing battle scene from the nearby shores. The day's action began at about 8:00 A.M. Just as the *Virginia* opened fire on the grounded *Minnesota*, the *Monitor*— the "Yankee cheese box on a raft"—appeared in Hampton Roads.

In a back and forth battle, the *Monitor* and *Virginia* then waged a duel that stunned the surprised onlookers. After repeated shots were fired by both vessels, *Monitor*'s attempt to ram *Virginia* failed. *Monitor* then sailed to

shallower waters to restock its ammunition supplies. Thinking that *Monitor* had run aground, *Virginia* opened fire on *Minnesota*, hoping to destroy the ship for good. Within minutes, *Monitor* was back in action and the two ironclads tried to ram each other.

Finally, *Merrimac* let loose with a blast that tore into *Monitor*, seriously injuring its commander, John Worden. Moments later, *Monitor* withdrew from the fight under new commander, Lieutenant Samuel Dana Greene.

In a last attempt to destroy *Minnesota*, *Virginia* steamed toward the battered ship. But at the last minute, the attack was called off and *Virginia* sailed away from the battle, ending one of America's most historic days of fighting.

THE MONITOR VS THE MERRIMAC

STEPHEN RUSSELL MALLORY WAS THE CONFEDERATE SECRETARY OF THE NAVY. HE WAS INTERESTED IN NEW SHIP TECHNOLOGIES, ESPECIALLY IRONCLAD WARSHIPS.

MR. PORTER, I NEED YOU TO BUILD A FLEET OF IRONCLADS TO DEFEND OUR SHIPPING AGAINST THE UNION BLOCKADE.

I SUGGEST WE RAISE *MERRIMAC* AND GIVE HER AN IRON HULL, MR. SECRETARY.

BEFORE LEAVING THEIR NAVAL BASE AT NORFOLK, VIRGINIA, UNION FORCES BURNED OUT AND SCUTTLED THEIR FRIGATE, USS *MERRIMAC*.

THE CONFEDERATE NAVY TOOK OVER THE BASE. THEY REBUILT THE VESSEL INTO AN IRON-COVERED WARSHIP.

AFTER EIGHT MONTHS OF WORK, MERRIMAC WAS RENAMED CSS *VIRGINIA*.

LIEUTENANT JONES, IN TWO DAYS WE WILL SAIL TO NEWPORT NEWS TO ATTACK THE UNION BLOCKADE.

A WEEK LATER, FLAG OFFICER FRANKLIN BUCHANAN TOOK COMMAND OF THE FIRST CONFEDERATE IRONCLAD WARSHIP.

BUT, SIR, THE SHIP HAS NO GUNPORT SHUTTERS, AND AMMUNITION FOR THE GUNS HAS ONLY JUST ARRIVED. BUILDING HAS NOT EVEN BEGUN BELOW DECKS.

BLUE SPEECH BALLOONS REPRESENT ACTUAL DIALOG

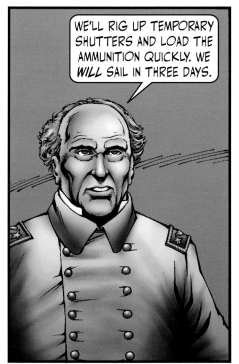

WE'LL RIG UP TEMPORARY SHUTTERS AND LOAD THE AMMUNITION QUICKLY. WE *WILL* SAIL IN THREE DAYS.

WE HAVEN'T EVEN TESTED OUR ENGINES, AND NONE OF THE GUNS HAVE BEEN FIRED. WE HAVEN'T MADE ANY SEA TRIALS.

ANYTHING COULD HAPPEN!

UNION SECRETARY OF THE NAVY GIDEON WELLES LEARNED THAT THE CONFEDERATES WERE BUILDING AN IRONCLAD WARSHIP.

WE MUST BUILD NEW SHIPS, TOO, MR. ERICSSON, IF WE ARE TO BEAT THE REBELS OUT OF THE OCEAN.

THE IRONCLAD I PLAN WE BUILD HAS NO MASTS OR SAILS, SECRETARY WELLES, SO THE GUN TURRETS CAN REVOLVE AND FIRE IN ANY DIRECTION.

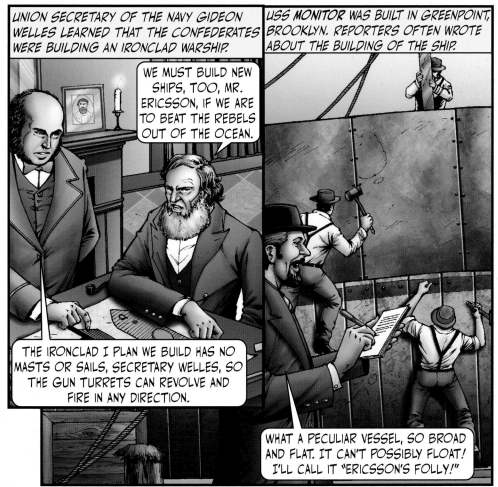

USS *MONITOR* WAS BUILT IN GREENPOINT, BROOKLYN. REPORTERS OFTEN WROTE ABOUT THE BUILDING OF THE SHIP.

WHAT A PECULIAR VESSEL, SO BROAD AND FLAT. IT CAN'T POSSIBLY FLOAT! I'LL CALL IT "ERICSSON'S FOLLY!"

VIRGINIA SAILED UP THE ELIZABETH RIVER ON SATURDAY, MARCH 8, 1862.

SIR, WE'RE HAVING TROUBLE STEERING. THE ENGINES ARE NOT PROVING RELIABLE.

VERY WELL, JONES. I'LL REQUEST A TOW FROM THE TUGS. SEND WORD TO *BEAUFORT* AND *RALEIGH.*

THE TWO TUGS KEPT THE GREAT IRONCLAD WARSHIP ON COURSE TO THE UNION BLOCKADE AT HAMPTON ROADS, VIRGINIA.

EARLIER, ON MARCH 4, LIEUTENANT JOHN WORDEN, COMMANDER OF *MONITOR*, RECEIVED HIS ORDERS.

WE ARE TO SAIL SOUTH TO THE HAMPTON ROADS BLOCKADE AS SOON AS POSSIBLE!

MONITOR WAS MOORED AT THE BROOKLYN NAVY YARD IN NEW YORK. THERE WAS A STORM THAT DAY, AND MONITOR WAS UNABLE TO SAIL.

ON MARCH 6, MONITOR WAS TOWED OUT OF NEW YORK BY THE THE TUGBOAT *SETH LOW*. THEY WERE ACCOMPANIED BY TWO GUNSHIPS, *CURRITUCK* AND *SACHEM*.

ENGINEER JOHN ERICSSON HAD DESIGNED *MONITOR* TO SAIL IN SHALLOW WATER, CLOSE TO THE COAST. IT WAS NOT DESIGNED TO SAIL IN OCEANS.

LIEUTENANT WORDEN WENT UP TO THE TURRET ON DECK TO GET FRESH AIR.

WILL THIS SEASICKNESS *NEVER* END?

THE WEATHER GOT STEADILY WORSE. LIEUTENANT WORDEN WENT BELOW DECKS. *MONITOR* WAS ALMOST ENGULFED BY THE WAVES.

MONITOR WAS CAUGHT IN A GALE. THE TURRET WAS NOT WATERTIGHT, AND WATER POURED INTO THE SHIP.

THE WATER GOT INTO THE ENGINE ROOM. IT CAUSED THE FANS TO STOP WORKING.

THE ENGINE ROOM FILLED WITH DANGEROUS FUMES. *MONITOR'S* CHIEF ENGINEER, ISAAC NEWTON, HAD TO WORK FAST.

SAILOR! LET'S GET TO WORK!

MEANWHILE, ON HIS *VIRGINIA*, BUCHANAN WAS SPEAKING TO ENGINEER H. ASHTON RAMSAY.

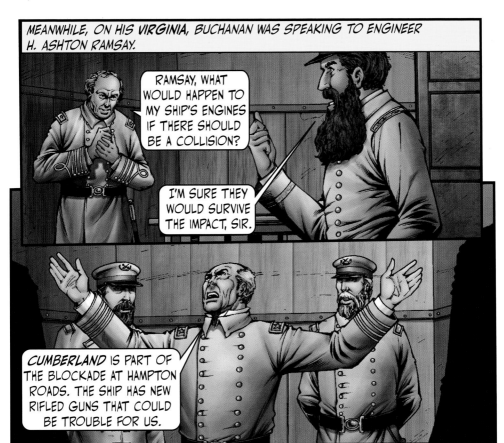

RAMSAY, WHAT WOULD HAPPEN TO MY SHIP'S ENGINES IF THERE SHOULD BE A COLLISION?

I'M SURE THEY WOULD SURVIVE THE IMPACT, SIR.

CUMBERLAND IS PART OF THE BLOCKADE AT HAMPTON ROADS. THE SHIP HAS NEW RIFLED GUNS THAT COULD BE TROUBLE FOR US.

RIFLED GUNS HAD SPIRAL GROOVES INSIDE THEIR BARRELS. THESE GROOVES MADE THE GUNS FIRE MORE ACCURATELY AND WITH GREATER FORCE THAN OTHER TYPES OF GUNS.

VIRGINIA WAS FITTED WITH A 1,500-POUND RAM AT ITS BOW. FLAG OFFICER BUCHANAN INTENDED TO MAKE FULL USE OF IT.

"I AM GOING TO RAM THE *CUMBERLAND*. I AM GOING TO MAKE RIGHT FOR HER AND RAM HER!" HE SAID.

THE UNION BLOCKADE AT HAMPTON ROADS INCLUDED SIXTY VESSELS. SOME OF THE SHIPS WERE SMALL CONVERTED RIVERBOATS. SOME OF THEM WERE SUPPLY BOATS AND OTHER CRAFT THAT WERE NOT ARMED.

UNION WARSHIPS, INCLUDING *CUMBERLAND* AND *CONGRESS*, WERE ALSO PART OF THE EFFECTIVE BLOCKADE.

CONGRESS HAD 50 SMOOTHBORE GUNS.* *CUMBERLAND* HAD 22 NINE-INCH SMOOTHBORE GUNS, AS WELL AS THE 170-POUND RIFLED GUN.

*THE INSIDE OF THE BARRELS OF SMOOTHBORE GUNS WERE SMOOTH. SMOOTHBORES WERE LESS EFFECTIVE THAN RIFLED GUNS.

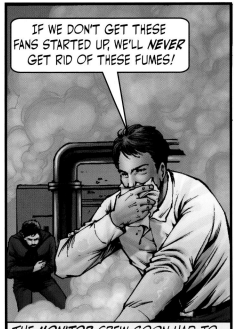

IF WE DON'T GET THESE FANS STARTED UP, WE'LL *NEVER* GET RID OF THESE FUMES!

THE *MONITOR* CREW SOON HAD TO ABANDON THE ENGINE ROOM. THE SHIP WAS TOWED INTO CALMER WATERS TO PREVENT IT FROM SINKING.

THE FANS ARE FINALLY WORKING, LT. WORDEN. WE'VE RESTARTED THE ENGINES AND THE PUMPS.

WONDERFUL NEWS, NEWTON. WE SET SAIL IMMEDIATELY.

MONITOR RESUMED ITS JOURNEY AT 8:00 P.M. ON FRIDAY, MARCH 7.

I'M NOT SURE WE SHOULD SAIL, SIR. THE SEA LEVEL IS UP AND WATER IS STILL COMING IN.

THEN PLUG UP THE HOLE, LT. GREENE, AND STOP THESE LEAKS!

THAT NIGHT, *MONITOR* HIT HEAVY STORMS AGAIN. UNABLE TO STEER IN THE WORSENING WEATHER, *MONITOR* ROLLED DANGEROUSLY. SHE WAS AT RISK OF CAPSIZING.

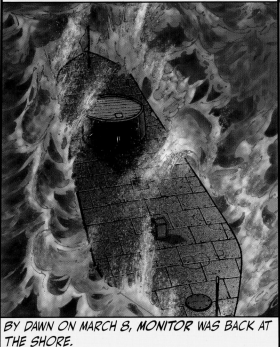

BY DAWN ON MARCH 8, *MONITOR* WAS BACK AT THE SHORE.

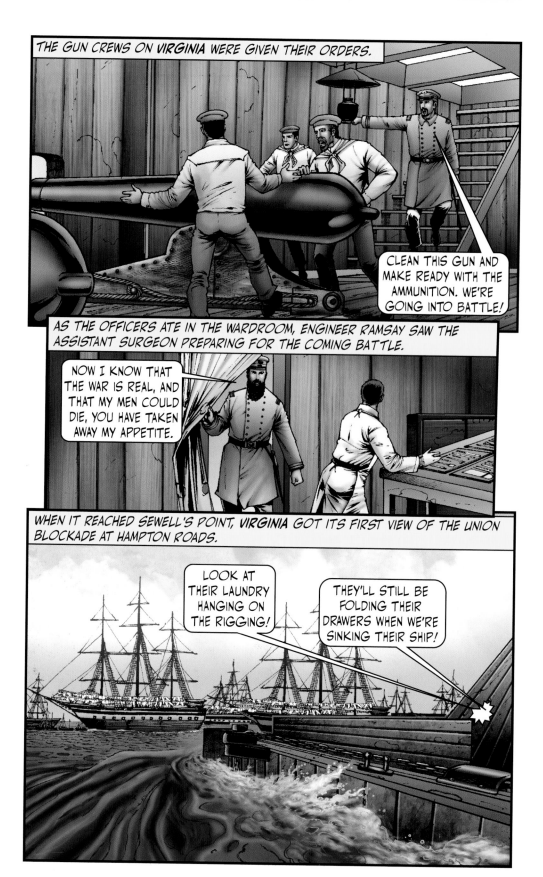

THE GUN CREWS ON **VIRGINIA** WERE GIVEN THEIR ORDERS.

CLEAN THIS GUN AND MAKE READY WITH THE AMMUNITION. WE'RE GOING INTO BATTLE!

AS THE OFFICERS ATE IN THE WARDROOM, ENGINEER RAMSAY SAW THE ASSISTANT SURGEON PREPARING FOR THE COMING BATTLE.

NOW I KNOW THAT THE WAR IS REAL, AND THAT MY MEN COULD DIE, YOU HAVE TAKEN AWAY MY APPETITE.

WHEN IT REACHED SEWELL'S POINT, **VIRGINIA** GOT ITS FIRST VIEW OF THE UNION BLOCKADE AT HAMPTON ROADS.

LOOK AT THEIR LAUNDRY HANGING ON THE RIGGING!

THEY'LL STILL BE FOLDING THEIR DRAWERS WHEN WE'RE SINKING THEIR SHIP!

THE FRENCH GUNBOAT *GASSENDI* WAS IN THE AREA TO OBSERVE THE BLOCKADE. CAPTAIN ANGE SIMON GAUTIER HAD ALREADY SEEN *VIRGINIA* IN NORFOLK.

THE FRENCH WOULD TAKE NO PART IN THE BATTLE OF HAMPTON ROADS, BUT WERE VERY INTERESTED IN THE NEW IRONCLAD WARSHIPS.

VIRGINIA HAS BEEN SIGHTED IN THE RIVER, CAPTAIN GAUTIER.

MAKE READY TO LEAVE. IF *VIRGINIA* IS ON HER WAY, THIS COULD BE A MOST INTERESTING DAY.

TELEGRAM THIS TO NEWPORT NEWS POINT. THE FRENCH ARE GETTING OUT OF THE LINE OF FIRE. THEY MUST KNOW THAT THE CONFEDERATES ARE ABOUT TO ATTACK US.

FROM FORT MONROE, UNION MAJOR GENERAL JOHN E. WOOL COULD SEE THE FRENCH GUNBOAT.

17

ON THE TUGBOAT USS *ZOUAVE*, ACTING MASTER HENRY REANY WAS KEEPING WATCH ON DECK.

MAKE FOR THE *CUMBERLAND*. THERE'S BLACK SMOKE IN THE ELIZABETH RIVER!

LT. SELFRIDGE! SOMETHING IS COMING UP THE RIVER!

MAKE HASTE AND INVESTIGATE, REANY. WE NEED TO KNOW IF WE ARE COMING UNDER ATTACK.

IS THAT *MERRIMAC?* IT LOOKS LIKE A BARN ROOF WITH A CHIMNEY FIRE!

AT 1:20 P.M. ON MARCH 8, *ZOUAVE* FIRED THE FIRST SHOTS OF THE BATTLE OF HAMPTON ROADS.

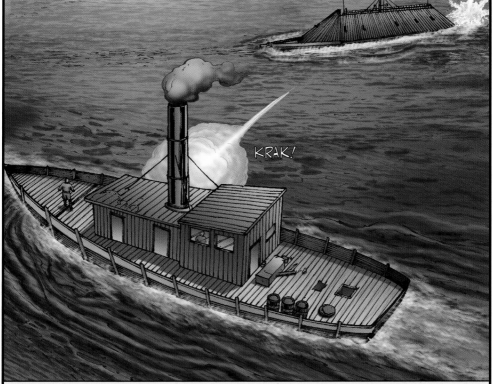

KRAK!

THE LITTLE TUGBOAT THEN TURNED AROUND AND HEADED BACK TO NEWPORT NEWS. THE STAGE WAS SET FOR A BATTLE THAT WOULD FOREVER CHANGE WAR AT SEA.

SUDDENLY, HAMPTON ROADS BURST INTO GREAT ACTIVITY. *CONGRESS* RAISED ITS SAILS AND *CUMBERLAND* TORE DOWN ITS WASHING LINES. SMALLER VESSELS SAILED FOR COVER.

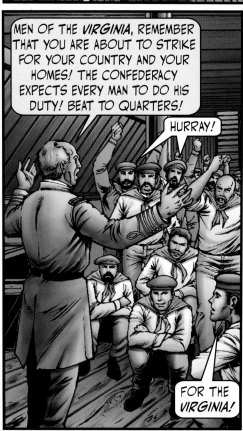

MEN OF THE *VIRGINIA*, REMEMBER THAT YOU ARE ABOUT TO STRIKE FOR YOUR COUNTRY AND YOUR HOMES! THE CONFEDERACY EXPECTS EVERY MAN TO DO HIS DUTY! BEAT TO QUARTERS!

HURRAY!

FOR THE *VIRGINIA!*

ON *CONGRESS*, ACTING COMMANDER JOSEPH B. SMITH ALSO GAVE A SPEECH.

MY HEARTIES, YOU SEE BEFORE YOU THE GREAT SOUTHERN BUGA-BOO, GOT UP TO FRIGHTEN US OUT OF OUR WITS! LET ME ASSURE YOU THAT ONE GOOD BROADSIDE FROM OUR GALLANT FRIGATE AND SHE IS OURS!

AT 2:00 P.M. **BEAUFORT** FIRED THE FIRST CONFEDERATE SHOTS. THE SHOTS FELL SHORT OF THEIR TARGET.

AS **VIRGINIA** SURGED FORWARD, **BEAUFORT** STAYED BACK. THE TUGBOAT COULD NOT DEFEND ITSELF AGAINST THE MIGHTY UNION WARSHIPS.

CONGRESS WATCHED THE ENEMY COME.

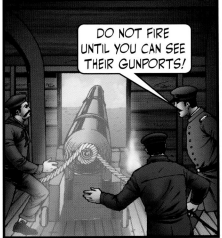

DO NOT FIRE UNTIL YOU CAN SEE THEIR GUNPORTS!

CONGRESS FIRED HER WEAPONS FROM ABOUT 550 YARDS. THE SHOT BOUNCED OFF THE IRONCLAD WARSHIP.

AT 2:20 P.M., **VIRGINIA** FIRED A ROUND OF GRAPESHOT FROM HER FORWARD GUN, STRAIGHT INTO **CONGRESS**.

THE SHOTS KILLED OR WOUNDED A DOZEN MEN.

FIRE!

KRAK! KRAK! BOOM!

THE SHOT PINGED AND BOUNCED OFF THE ARMORED SURFACE OF *VIRGINIA*. THE IRONCLAD SHIP SUFFERED NO DAMAGE.

CONGRESS FIRED ALL OF ITS GUNS ALONG ONE SIDE AT THE SAME TIME. THE BROADSIDE INCLUDED 25 GUNS. FIVE OF THEM WERE THE NEWLY DESIGNED 8-INCH DAHLGREN SMOOTHBORES.

FROM 300 YARDS, *VIRGINIA* FIRED A STARBOARD BROADSIDE ON *CONGRESS*. THE WOODEN WARSHIP WAS RIPPED APART. MEN WERE KILLED AND THE GUNDECKS WERE DESTROYED.

VIRGINIA'S GUNS HAD BEEN LOADED WITH HEATED SHOT THAT BURNED THE WOODEN SURFACES OF *CONGRESS*.

BEFORE LONG, *CONGRESS* WAS ON FIRE. LARGE NUMBERS OF HER CREW WERE ALREADY DEAD.

EARLIER THAT DAY, *MONITOR* WAS STILL NEAR THE SHORE, WAITING FOR THE WEATHER TO CALM.

THAT'S CAPE CHARLES. WE'RE APPROACHING THE NORTH END OF THE CHESAPEAKE BAY.

MONITOR HAD ALMOST SUNK TWICE, BUT WITH NOT FAR TO GO, ITS MAIDEN VOYAGE WAS COMING TO AN END.

AT NOON THE SHIP FINALLY CONTINUED ITS JOURNEY TOWARD HAMPTON ROADS.

DURING THE AFTERNOON, *MONITOR'S* CREW SAW BLACK SMOKE AND FLASHES OF GUNS IN THE SKY.

THE BATTLE IS ALREADY RAGING. TOO BAD WE CAN'T MOVE ANY FASTER. NEVERTHELESS, WE *MUST* PREPARE TO ENGAGE THE ENEMY!

VIRGINIA PASSED WITHIN YARDS OF CONGRESS.

THEY'RE GOING TO SEND A BOARDING PARTY!

MCKEAN BUCHANAN, PAYMASTER ON *CONGRESS*, SURVIVED THE BROADSIDE. FRANKLIN BUCHANAN, WHO COMMANDED *VIRGINIA*, WAS HIS BROTHER.

THIS WAS A WAR THAT NOT ONLY DIVIDED A NATION, BUT ALSO DIVIDED FAMILIES.

WE'RE DOOMED!

I'VE NEVER SEEN ANYTHING LIKE IT! SHE'S GOING TO COME AT US AGAIN WITH A *PORT BROADSIDE!*

NO! LOOK! I THINK SHE'S PASSING US!

LT. SMITH, ONBOARD *CONGRESS* ...

CALL FOR *ZOUAVE* TO TOW US, AND CUT THE ANCHOR CABLES. I'LL BEACH THIS SHIP, RATHER THAN SEE IT SINK!

CONGRESS' CREW BEGAN TO FIGHT THE FIRES. *VIRGINIA* DID NOT FIRE ON *CONGRESS* AGAIN.

DR. EDWARD SHIPPEN, SURGEON ON *CONGRESS*, TENDED TO THE WOUNDED.

WITH SO MANY DEAD IT IS A MARVEL THERE ARE ANY WOUNDED TO HEAL.

LT. SMITH BEACHED *CONGRESS* IN SEVENTEEN FEET OF WATER. ALTHOUGH NO LONGER SEAWORTHY, THE SHIP COULD STILL FIGHT.

VIRGINIA CONTINUED TOWARD *CUMBERLAND*, THREATENING TO ATTACK.

CUMBERLAND FIRED ITS GUNS FIRST. THE FOREWARD GUNS AND 150-POUND RIFLE HAD ALMOST NO EFFECT ON *VIRGINIA*.

VIRGINIA FIRED ITS BOW GUNS ON *CUMBERLAND*, RIPPING INTO THE SIDE OF THE WOODEN WARSHIP.

WHILE ATTACKING *CUMBERLAND*, *VIRGINIA* STILL HAD TO DEFEND ITS FLANK. A GUN BATTLE STARTED BETWEEN *VIRGINIA'S* STARBOARD GUNS AND THE UNION BATTERY AT NEWPORT NEWS POINT.

ONBOARD *CUMBERLAND*, MEN WERE SUFFERING AND DYING.

TAKE COURAGE MEN, AND MAN THOSE GUNS!

THERE WERE STILL NO CASUALTIES ON *VIRGINIA*. GUNS CONTINUED TO FIRE ON *CUMBERLAND* AND THE UNION BATTERY.

FIRE!

THE FRENCH OBSERVERS ON *GASSENDI* SAW MORE THAN THEY COULD EVER HAVE HOPED FOR. *VIRGINIA* WAS FIGHTING ON TWO FLANKS, WHILE TAKING LITTLE OR NO DAMAGE.

THE FORCE OF THE FIRE IS *INCREDIBLE!* WHAT AN *EXTRAORDINARY* BATTLE!

AFTER CONFIRMING HIS ENGINES WOULD SURVIVE, BUCHANAN GAVE THE SIGNAL TO RAM *CUMBERLAND*. THE ENGINES WERE CUT OFF AND THE CREW WAS WARNED OF THE COMING CRASH.

STAND FAST! WE'RE GOING TO RUN INTO *CUMBERLAND*!

AT 3:05 P.M., *VIRGINIA* DROVE STRAIGHT INTO *CUMBERLAND* WITH ITS 1,500-POUND RAM, SMASHING THROUGH ITS HULL WITH A MIGHTY FORCE.

CUMBERLAND CONTINUED TO FIRE ITS GUNS, DESPITE BEING BADLY CRIPPLED AND TAKING ON WATER.

THE TWO SHIPS WERE LOCKED TOGETHER IN BATTLE.

CUMBERLAND FIRED THREE FAST BROADSIDES INTO *VIRGINIA*.

FIRE!

VIRGINIA WAS DAMAGED WHEN THE MUZZLES OF TWO OF ITS GUNS WERE DESTROYED.

VIRGINIA'S SMOKESTACK WAS HIT BY A SHELL. IT CAUSED A TERRIBLE CRASH IN THE FIRE ROOM.

HURRAY!

BRAVO!

WE GOT HER AT LAST!

WE'RE SURE TO GO DOWN, BUT AT LEAST WE'LL TAKE THEM WITH US!

BUT VIRGINIA DID NOT GO DOWN WITH CUMBERLAND. AT 3:15 P.M., AFTER LEAVING ITS RAM BEHIND, VIRGINIA MANAGED TO BACK AWAY FROM THE ENEMY.

THE HOLE IN *CUMBERLAND* WAS BIG ENOUGH TO DRIVE A HORSE AND CART THROUGH. WATER QUICKLY POURED INTO THE SHIP.

AAARRGH! NO!

HELP US!

MOST OF THE WOUNDED ON *CUMBERLAND* WERE DOOMED TO DEATH BY DROWNING.

EVEN AS IT WAS SINKING, *CUMBERLAND* CONTINUED TO FIRE ON THE DREADED *VIRGINIA*.

UNION ARTILLERY BATTERIES ON THE SHORE FIRED AGAIN AND AGAIN ON *VIRGINIA*. BUT THE SHOTS CONTINUED TO BOUNCE OFF ITS HULL.

WHEN *VIRGINIA* AGAIN RAMMED *CUMBERLAND* AT 3:15 P.M., THE UNION SHIP GOT IN A LAST LUCKY SHOT. IT MANAGED TO TAKE OUT THE BOW GUN ON THE IRONCLAD, KILLING TWO CREW MEMBERS.

THEY WERE THE FIRST CASUALTIES ON AN IRONCLAD WARSHIP.

DURING THE RAMMING, THE JAMES RIVER SQUADRON OF CONFEDERATE VESSELS WAS ABLE TO MOVE INTO POSITION CLOSE TO SEWELL'S POINT.

UNION SHIPS ALSO TRIED TO GET INTO POSITION FOR BATTLE, BUT *MINNESOTA* AND *ST. LAWRENCE* RAN AGROUND. THEY WOULD NOT BE ABLE TO MOVE FOR SIX HOURS, BUT THEY WERE IN A GOOD DEFENSIVE POSITION.

AT 3:20 P.M., *CUMBERLAND* SANK.

4:10 P.M. *VIRGINIA* ATTACKED THE BEACHED *CONGRESS* FOR A SECOND TIME.

AFTER 50 MINUTES, WITH THEIR SHIP ON FIRE AND THEIR MEN WOUNDED AND DYING, THE OFFICERS ON *CONGRESS* RAISED TWO FLAGS OF SURRENDER.

NOW CSS **BEAUFORT** MOVED IN TO RESCUE THE SURVIVORS ON BOARD **CONGRESS** AND TO TAKE THEM PRISONER. HOWEVER, THE UNION BATTERIES DID NOT SUPPORT THE SHIP'S SURRENDER AND FIRED ON **BEAUFORT**.

SEEING **BEAUFORT** BEING FIRED UPON, FLAG OFFICER BUCHANAN WAS FURIOUS.

PLUG HOT SHOT INTO HER AND DON'T LEAVE HER UNTIL SHE'S AFIRE!

SUDDENLY, BUCHANAN WAS HIT BY A RIFLE BULLET, AND HAD TO BE CARRIED TO SAFETY.

THAT SHIP MUST BE BURNED! THEY MUST LOOK AFTER THEIR OWN WOUNDED, SINCE THEY WON'T LET US!

DR. SHIPPEN AND MCKEAN BUCHANAN BOTH SURVIVED THE DESTRUCTION OF **CONGRESS**.

HOWEVER, MCKEAN'S BROTHER, FRANKLIN, HAD BEEN BADLY INJURED AS COMMANDER OF THE IRONCLAD **VIRGINIA**.

UNDER THE COMMAND OF LIEUTENANT JONES, **VIRGINIA** RETIRED TO SEWELL POINT AT 6:30 P.M. THE IRONCLAD WOULD BE PROTECTED BY THE CONFEDERATE BATTERY STATIONED THERE.

AT 7:45 P.M., FLAG OFFICER BUCHANAN WAS TAKEN OFF **VIRGINIA**, ALONG WITH THE CAPTURED UNION WOUNDED AND PRISONERS. ABOUT 260 SAILORS WERE KILLED. ALMOST AS MANY WERE WOUNDED.

NEARLY ALL THE DEAD AND WOUNDED WERE UNION SAILORS.

CONGRESS BURNED INTO THE NIGHT AND FINALLY EXPLODED AT 12:30 A.M., WHEN MONITOR ARRIVED AT HAMPTON ROADS.

A PILOT ON **VIRGINIA** CLAIMED TO HAVE SEEN "THE ERICSSON," BUT RUMORS OF ITS ARRIVAL WERE DISMISSED AS NONSENSE BY THE CONFEDERATES.

DAWN, MARCH 9. MINNESOTA WAS THE BIGGEST THREAT TO VIRGINIA ON DAY TWO OF THE BATTLE. ITS CREW REMOVED ALL EXTRA WEIGHT TO MAKE MINNESOTA AS LIGHT AS POSSIBLE.

LIEUTENANT JAMES HENRY ROCHELLE ON CSS PATRICK HENRY WAS ONE OF THE FIRST TO SPOT MONITOR.

WHAT IS THAT STRANGE VESSEL?

LIEUTENANT JONES RECOGNIZED MONITOR.

THAT'S MONITOR, THE UNION IRONCLAD. WE MUST ATTACK HER, RAM HER, AND KEEP VIGOROUSLY AT HER UNTIL THIS CONTEST IS DECIDED!

8:00 A.M., MARCH 9. VIRGINIA, ESCORTED BY PATRICK HENRY AND JAMESTOWN, SET SAIL TOWARD MINNESOTA.

CAPTAIN JACQUES VAN BRUNT OF *MINNESOTA* SPOKE WITH WORDEN ON *MONITOR* BEFORE THE SHIPS WENT INTO BATTLE.

IF I CANNOT LIGHTEN MY SHIP OFF, I WILL DESTROY HER!

I WILL STAND BY YOU TO THE LAST IF I CAN HELP YOU!

GET THE SHIP UNDERWAY AS QUICKLY AS POSSIBLE. WE MUST ENGAGE THE CONFEDERATE IRONCLAD AS FAR AWAY FROM *MINNESOTA* AS POSSIBLE.

THE COMMUNICATION LINK BETWEEN THE GUN TURRET AND THE PILOT HOUSE HAD BEEN LOST. TWO SAILORS HAD TO RELAY MESSAGES BETWEEN WORDEN IN THE PILOT HOUSE AND HIS GUNNERS IN THE TURRET.

TELL MR. GREENE NOT TO FIRE TIL I GIVE THE WORD, TO BE COOL AND DELIBERATE, TO TAKE SURE AIM AND NOT TO WASTE A SHOT!

THERE IS DISPUTE OVER WHO FIRED THE FIRST SHOTS OF THE GREAT BATTLE. SOME SAY IT WAS THE GUNBOATS ACCOMPANYING *VIRGINIA*. OTHERS CLAIM IT WAS *MINNESOTA* THAT OPENED FIRE FIRST.

TO PROTECT *MINNESOTA* FROM CONFEDERATE GUNFIRE, *MONITOR* ATTACKED *VIRGINIA*, GUNS BLAZING.

PATRICK HENRY AND *JAMESTOWN* RETREATED FROM THE ENGAGEMENT. THEY RETURNED TO SEWELL POINT, LEAVING *VIRGINIA* TO TAKE ON *MONITOR* ALONE.

SOLDIERS AND SAILORS ON BOTH SIDES OF THE CONFLICT WATCHED IN AMAZEMENT AS TWO GREAT IRONCLAD WARSHIPS JOINED BATTLE FOR THE FIRST TIME IN HISTORY.

WORDEN LATER DESCRIBED HIS CONCERNS ABOUT *MONITOR*...

"I FELT SOME ANXIETY ABOUT THE TURRET MACHINERY, IT HAVING BEEN PREDICTED BY MANY THAT A HEAVY SHOT STRIKING THE TURRET WOULD SO DERANGE IT AS TO STOP ITS WORKING. IT HAD BEEN STRUCK TWICE AND STILL REVOLVED AS FREELY AS EVER."

"I TURNED BACK WITH RENEWED HOPE AND CONTINUED TO ENGAGE THE *VIRGINIA* AT CLOSE QUARTERS; EVERY SHOT STRIPPING OFF THE IRON FREELY."

AFTER THE SUCCESS OF THE FIRST DAY'S BATTLE, *VIRGINIA* HAD MET HER MATCH.

CAPTAIN JOHN A. DAHLGREN HAD DESIGNED *MONITOR'S* GUNS. BECAUSE THEY HAD NOT BEEN TESTED, HE SUGGESTED THEY ONLY USE TWO-THIRDS OF THE NORMAL CHARGE FOR THE GUNS – IN CASE THEY PROVED UNSAFE.

IF I COULD ONLY USE THE FULL CHARGE IN THE GUNS, I BET WE COULD BREAK *VIRGINIA'S* HULL!

VIRGINIA'S CHIEF ENGINEER, ASHTON RAMSAY, ALSO HAD PROBLEMS WITH AMMUNITION.

HAD WE KNOWN OF *MONITOR*, WE COULD HAVE STORED SOLID SHOT FOR OUR RIFLED CANNON.

ALL WE HAVE ARE PERCUSSIVE SHELLS, WHICH MIGHT NOT PENETRATE OUR ENEMY'S DEFENSES!

I MIGHT NOT BE ABLE TO DEFEAT THE IRONCLAD, BUT I CAN STILL DESTROY *MINNESOTA!*

VIRGINIA IS STILL A DANGEROUS ENEMY. I CANNOT ALLOW THEM TO ATTACK *MINNESOTA.*

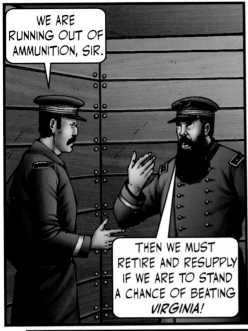

WE ARE RUNNING OUT OF AMMUNITION, SIR.

THEN WE MUST RETIRE AND RESUPPLY IF WE ARE TO STAND A CHANCE OF BEATING *VIRGINIA!*

MONITOR IS RETREATING!

THIS IS OUR CHANCE TO ATTACK *MINNESOTA*.

AT A DISTANCE OF TWO MILES FROM *MINNESOTA*, *VIRGINIA* ACCIDENTALLY GOT STUCK ON THE RIVERBED.

RAMSAY TOOK DESPERATE MEASURES TO FREE HIS SHIP. TO GET EXTRA POWER, HE HAD THE CREW STOKE THE BOILER TO DANGEROUS LEVELS.

VIRGINIA CALLED ON GUNBOATS *JAMESTOWN* AND *PATRICK HENRY* TO TOW IT BACK INTO DEEP WATER. THE TWO GUNBOATS SLOWLY BEGAN THEIR APPROACH.

WITH *VIRGINIA* BACK IN OPEN WATER, *JAMESTOWN* AND *PATRICK HENRY* QUICKLY RETREATED TO SAFETY.

WE HAVE BEEN FIRING ON *MONITOR* FOR TWO HOURS, SIR, BUT WE HAVE NOT YET DAMAGED IT.

THEN WE MUST THINK OF SOME OTHER WAY TO DESTROY THAT SHIP!

LOOK OUT NOW, I THINK THEY'RE GOING TO RUN US DOWN! GIVE THEM *BOTH* GUNS!

VIRGINIA STRUCK THE SIDE OF MONITOR, KNOCKING THE CREW OFF THEIR FEET AND SENDING THE UNION IRONCLAD SPINNING.

MONITOR WAS DENTED IN THE COLLISION, BUT VIRGINIA SUFFERED DAMAGE TO ITS BOW, CAUSING A LEAK.

THEN MONITOR'S GUNS SCORED A DIRECT HIT INTO THE STERN OF VIRGINIA. ANOTHER SHOT COULD BREACH VIRGINIA'S HULL.

FIRE, MEN! FIRE!

WE WILL BOARD MONITOR, BLIND THE PILOT HOUSE, AND JAM THE GUN TURRET AT THE SAME TIME!

ALTHOUGH CONFEDERATE CAPTAIN REUBEN T. THORN ORGANIZED A BOARDING PARTY, VIRGINIA STILL HAD FIGHT LEFT IN IT.

AS *MONITOR* PASSED THE STERN OF *VIRGINIA*, LIEUTENANT JOHN TAYLOR WOOD AIMED THE 7-INCH BROOKE RIFLE AT *MONITOR'S* PILOT HOUSE, AND FIRED.

HE SCORED A DIRECT HIT.

AARRGH! MY EYES! I CAN'T SEE!

LIEUTENANT SAMUEL DANA GREENE TOOK COMMAND FOR THE INJURED WORDEN.

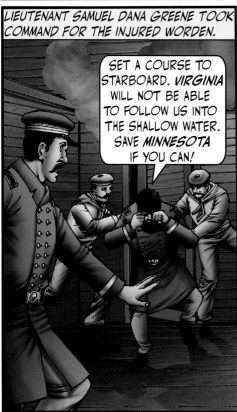

SET A COURSE TO STARBOARD. *VIRGINIA* WILL NOT BE ABLE TO FOLLOW US INTO THE SHALLOW WATER. SAVE *MINNESOTA* IF YOU CAN!

MONITOR IS WITHDRAWING. NOW WE CAN ATTACK *MINNESOTA*!

NO. WE CAN'T RISK GETTING STUCK IN THAT SHALLOW WATER AGAIN. THE SHIP IS LEAKING AND THE CREW IS EXHAUSTED.

IF WE DO NOT MAKE *MINNESOTA* SURRENDER, THEN WE CANNOT CLAIM A TRUE VICTORY.

WE HAVE DONE ENOUGH. WE WILL SET A COURSE FOR SEWELL'S POINT.

ALTHOUGH *VIRGINIA* HAD BEEN VICTORIOUS ON THE FIRST DAY OF THE BATTLE OF HAMPTON ROADS, IT COULD NOT CLAIM AN OVERALL VICTORY. NEVERTHELESS, WHEN THE SHIP RETURNED TO SEWELL'S POINT, IT WAS GREETED WITH A HERO'S WELCOME.

MONITOR RETURNED HOME TO A GRAND WELCOME FROM THE UNION TROOPS AT NEWPORT NEWS. ALTHOUGH *MONITOR* HAD NOT WON THE BATTLE, IT HAD SAVED THE DAY BY PREVENTING *VIRGINIA* FROM ATTACKING *MINNESOTA*.

THE END

This illustration shows the ramming of the USS *Cumberland* by the CSS *Virginia*. The *Cumberland* sank shortly after, taking many men with her. (Courtesy of Stratford Archive)

AFTERMATH

Each ironclad took and dished out plenty of punishment during the fighting, also called the Battle of Hampton Roads. *Monitor* was hit twenty-three times by *Virginia*'s blasts. *Virginia* was hit twenty times. Despite the damage, both ships survived. However, there was no clear victor.

The Union side claimed victory because the *Monitor* had effectively handled the threat posed by *Virginia*. *Monitor*'s performance also convinced the Union that *Virginia* could not break the Union blockade alone. Additionally, the North believed their superior industrial power would ensure that they would win a race to create more ironclad warships.

The Confederates claimed victory because *Virginia* had destroyed several Union warships on the first day of battle. *Virginia* also maintained control of the James River and posed a threat to the Union army at Fort Monroe. For that reason, the Union moved its base to the York River.

Several times over the next weeks, *Virginia* appeared in full view of the blockade. Each time, the wooden Union ships retreated to defensive positions, hoping not to be attacked. *Monitor* did not support the attempted attacks of its wooden warships, and whenever *Virginia* appeared, it too retreated. President Abraham Lincoln visited the area and was upset that *Monitor* was not more aggressive.

After a series of minor battles with Union forces, the Confederates destroyed and left Norfolk Navy Yard. The Confederate army was on the move, and the navy base was no longer a defensive priority. *Virginia* lost her base and could not be used near the Confederate capital at Richmond, Virginia, because the waters there were too shallow. On May 11, 1862, *Virginia* was destroyed.

Monitor remained in the area for several more months. Its next threat was the newly built Confederate ironclad, *Richmond*. *Monitor* was ordered to travel south to join the blockade at Wilmington, Delaware. The vessel was being towed there when it was struck by a storm. The first Union ironclad sank on December 31, 1862. Its remains still lie in 220 feet of water.

Not long after its fight with the *Monitor*, the CSS *Virginia* tried to escape back to Richmond, but got stuck in the James River. Her crew had to burn and abandon her. (Courtesy of Hensley)

Only nine months after its battle against *Virginia*, the USS *Monitor* sank in a gale off Cape Hatteras, on December 31, 1862. (Courtesy of HCA)

GLOSSARY

abandon   To leave forever; to give up.

aground   On or onto the shore or the bottom of a body of water.

blockade   The closing off of an area to prevent movement of people and supplies.

bow   The front part of a ship or boat.

broadside   The firing of all the guns on one side of a ship at the same time.

capsize   To overturn or cause to overturn.

convert   To make something into something else.

dismiss   To refuse to seriously consider.

engage   To take part or involve oneself.

engulf   To swallow up or cover completely by or as if by overflowing.

frigate   A warship with square sails.

hull   The body or frame of a ship or boat, including only its sides and bottom.

impact   The act of one object striking against another.

ironclad   An armored naval vessel of the mid- to late-nineteenth century.

muzzle   The front of a gun barrel.

scuttle   To sink or destroy a boat by making holes through its bottom.

starboard   The right-hand side of a ship.

stern   The rear part of a ship or boat.

turret   A structure on a tank or warship on which rotating guns are mounted.

FOR MORE INFORMATION

ORGANIZATIONS

The Mariners' Museum
100 Museum Drive
Newport News, VA 23606
USA
001 (757) 596-2222
Web site:
www.mariner.org/monitor/04_revunion/

National Civil War Museum
P.O. Box 1861
Harrisburg, PA 17105-1861
USA
001 (717) 260-1861

The turret of the USS *Monitor* was only 20 feet wide, and conditions were cramped, hot and dangerous. (Adam Hook © Osprey Publishing)

▼

FOR FURTHER READING

Anderson, Dale. *Civil War at Sea*. Milwaukee, WI: Gareth Stevens Audio, 2003.

Carter, Alden R. *Battle of the Ironclads: The Monitor and the Merrimack*. Danbury, CT: Scholastic Library Publishing, 1993.

Cunningham, Alvin Robert. Conrad Elroy, Powder Monkey: *The Role of the Navy in the Civil War*. Logan, IA: Perfection Learning Company, 2004.

Konstam, Angus. *Hampton Roads 1862: Clash of the Ironclads*. Oxford, England: Osprey Publishing, 2002.

Sappey, Maureen Stack. *Dreams of Ships, Dreams of Sea: At Sea With the Monitor and the Merrimac*. Shippensburg, PA: White Mane Publishing Company, Inc., 1998.

INDEX